82291

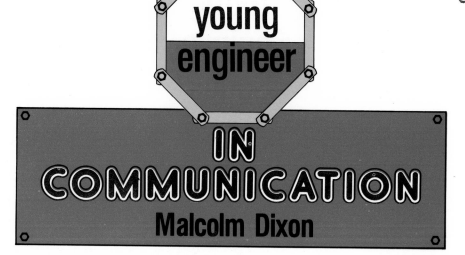

young engineer

IN COMMUNICATION

Malcolm Dixon

A Young Engineer Book

The Bookwright Press
New York · 1983

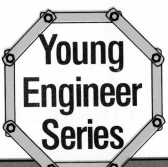

Young Engineer Series

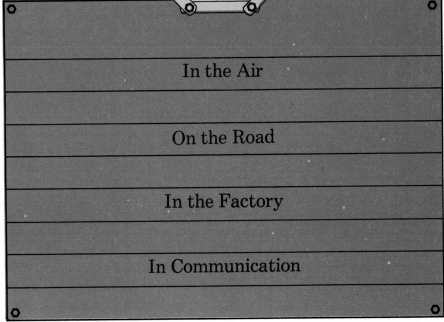

In the Air

On the Road

In the Factory

In Communication

First published in the United States in 1983 by
The Bookwright Press, 387 Park Avenue South,
New York, NY 10016
First published in 1982 by
Wayland Publishers Limited, England
ISBN: 0-531-04700-8
Library of Congress Catalog Card Number 83-71637
© Copyright 1982 by Wayland Publishers Limited
All rights reserved
Illustrated by Gerald Wood
Printed in Italy by G. Canale & C.S.p.A.

Contents

Sending messages

Without communication we would be isolated from each other. Babies cry and so pass information to their mothers. At school we learn to read and write, and listen and speak to others. Today we are also able to communicate over long distances. How many different types of communication can you think of?

Count the number of people you talk to in one day.
How much time do you spend watching television in one week?
How much time do you spend talking to friends on the telephone?
Listen to the news on the radio. Count the number of countries that are mentioned.

Communicating over vast distances

People live in different towns and cities scattered across the world. These communities are often separated by many miles and

by oceans and mountains. For hundreds of years people have tried to invent ways to communicate over these distances and barriers. We now live at a time when it is easy to communicate with a friend in the next town or across the world.

When astronauts traveled to another plant — the moon — we were even able to watch them as they walked on the surface. Engineers using complicated machinery have made it possible for us to communicate in this way.

Chapter 2

Simple communication

Semaphore

One way to send signals is to use two flags and a special code. This method is often used by sailors. It is called semaphore.

The flags are held in different positions for each letter of the alphabet.

Make two flags using handkerchiefs and pieces of wood. Hold each flag at arm's length. You are now signaling the letter 'R'.

R

Move your arms to signal other letters from the alphabet shown here How quickly can you signal the word 'READY'?

E   **A**   **D**   **Y**

Why do you think flags are used in this method of signaling?

Ask a friend to read your signals.

Can your friend read your signals over a long distance?

Nearly two hundred years ago semaphore towers were built. They used large moving wooden arms to send semaphore messages.

6   **The Semaphore code**

Using mirrors

Find a small mirror. Use it to reflect sunlight onto a wall. Move your mirror so that you are flashing spots of light onto the wall.
Cut a piece of cardboard a little larger than your mirror.
Use the cardboard to help flash the light on and off.
Can you invent a code to send messages?
One flash could stand for the letter A. Send two flashes for the letter B.
Try to signal your name.
Simple machines have been used to reflect sunlight and send messages. They are called heliographs and work in a similar way to your mirror method. These heliograph machines were often used by soldiers.
What happens when the sun is not shining?

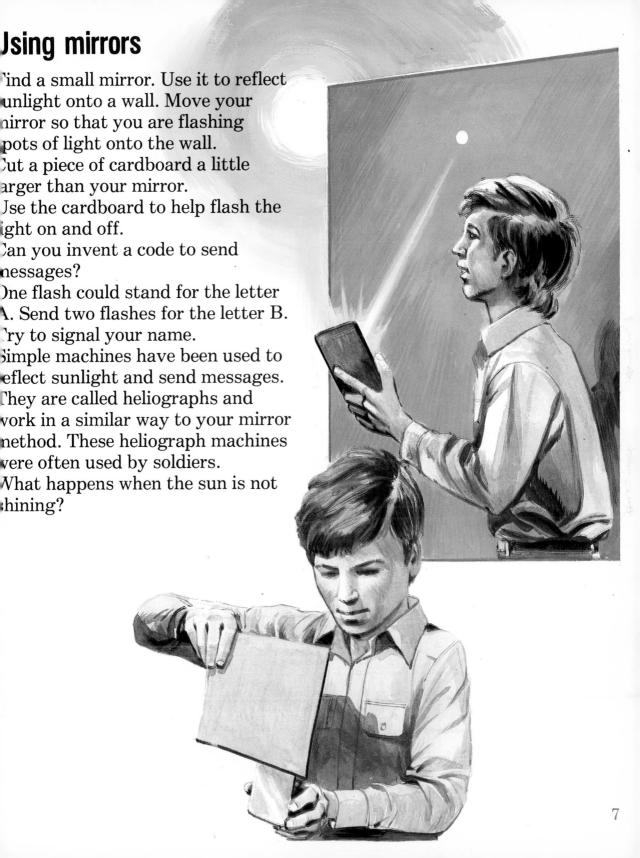

Vibrations

Position a flexible ruler on a table so most of it is over the edge. Hold one end of the ruler on the table and carefully pull down the other end. What happens when you let that end of the ruler go?

Look at the way the ruler moves rapidly up and down.
The ruler is vibrating.
Listen to the sound that it makes.

Now move the ruler so that only half of it is over the edge of the table.
Make the ruler vibrate.
Do these vibrations make the same sound as before?

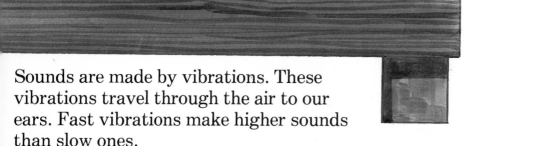

Sounds are made by vibrations. These vibrations travel through the air to our ears. Fast vibrations make higher sounds than slow ones.

8

Make a simple telephone

Find two empty yogurt containers. Make small holes in the bottom of each. Cut a length of string and thread each end through the holes in the containers. Tie a large knot inside each container.

Give one yogurt container to a friend. Tell your friend to put it close to his ear. Move away from your friend until the string between you is tight. Talk into your yogurt container.

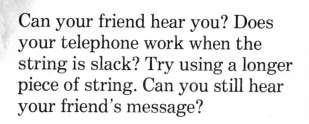

Can your friend hear you? Does your telephone work when the string is slack? Try using a longer piece of string. Can you still hear your friend's message?

When you speak into the yogurt container, the sound vibrations travel along the string. So your friend is able to hear your message.

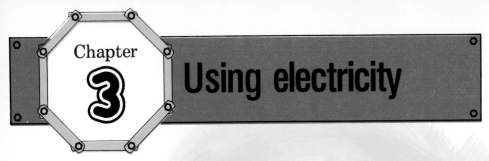

Using electricity

Chapter **3**

Bulbs, batteries and switches

Bulb socket

We can use electricity to send messages along wires.
But remember, **never use electric outlets. Strong current can kill**. Always use batteries for your experiments.
Screw a bulb into a bulb socket. Connect one side of the bulb-socket to a battery.

Find a small piece of wood, two thumbtacks and a paperclip.
Use these to make a switch. Connect the bulb socket to the switch, and the other side of the switch to the battery. Use the paperclip switch to complete the circuit.
Does the bulb light up?

Switch

Batter

Make a circuit using two longer wires. Can you still make the bulb go on and off?

Morse code

To help send messages you can use Morse code. This code uses dashes and dots (long and short flashes) for different letters of the alphabet.

A ·— E · I ··
B —··· F ··—· J ·———
C —·—· G ——· K —·—
D —·· H ···· L ·—··
M ——

N —· R ·—· V ···—
O ——— S ··· W ·——
P ·——· T — X —··—
Q ——·— U ··— Y —·——
Z ——··

Use your switch to send a message to a friend in Morse code. Your friend will need a copy of the code to read your message.

The Morse code for numbers

1 ·———— 4 ····— 7 ——···
2 ··——— 5 ····· 8 ———··
3 ···—— 6 —···· 9 ————·
0 —————

Try using a buzzer or a bell in your circuit. Can you think of a secret code of your own?

Sending signals

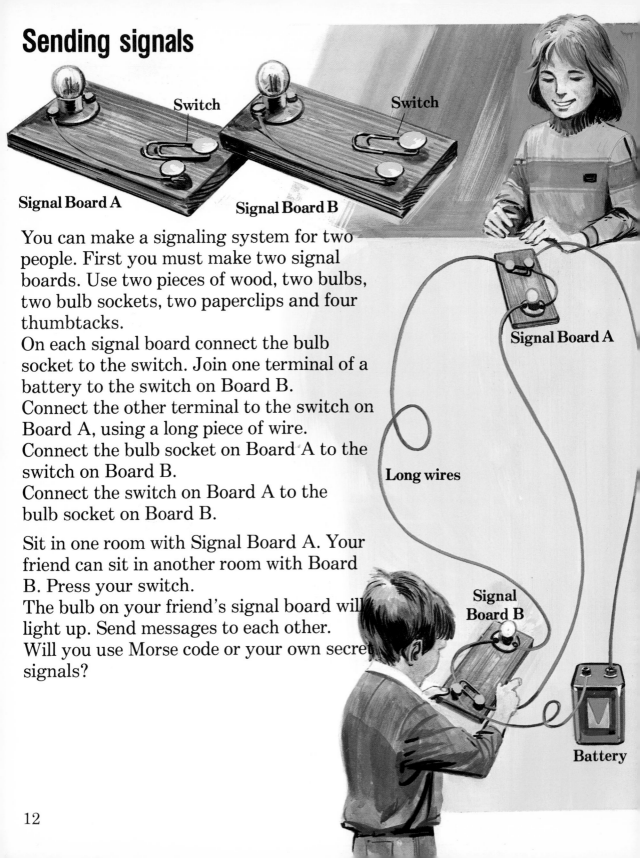

Signal Board A

Switch

Signal Board B

Switch

Signal Board A

Long wires

Signal Board B

Battery

You can make a signaling system for two people. First you must make two signal boards. Use two pieces of wood, two bulbs, two bulb sockets, two paperclips and four thumbtacks.

On each signal board connect the bulb socket to the switch. Join one terminal of a battery to the switch on Board B.

Connect the other terminal to the switch on Board A, using a long piece of wire.

Connect the bulb socket on Board A to the switch on Board B.

Connect the switch on Board A to the bulb socket on Board B.

Sit in one room with Signal Board A. Your friend can sit in another room with Board B. Press your switch.

The bulb on your friend's signal board will light up. Send messages to each other.

Will you use Morse code or your own secret signals?

Electromagnets

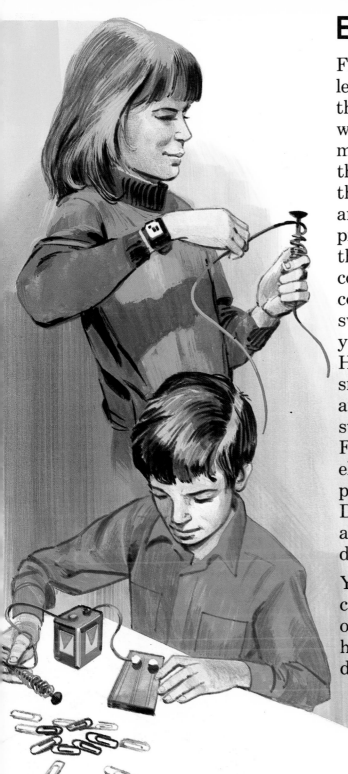

Find a large iron nail and a long length of fine, covered wire. Wind the wire around the nail. Always wind in the same direction. You may need to use some tape to hold the layers of wire in place. Connect the ends of the wire to a battery and a switch. The boy in the picture has connected one end of the wire to the battery. Now, to complete the circuit, he must connect the other end to the switch. Make this circuit just as you did on page 10.

Hold your electromagnet over a small pile of paperclips. Switch on and watch what happens. Now switch off. What happens?

From what distance does your electromagnet still attract the paperclips?

Does the number of turns of wire around the nail make any difference?

You have made a magnet that you can control by switching it on and off. Electromagnets, as we will see, help us to communicate over long distances.

Make a telegraph system

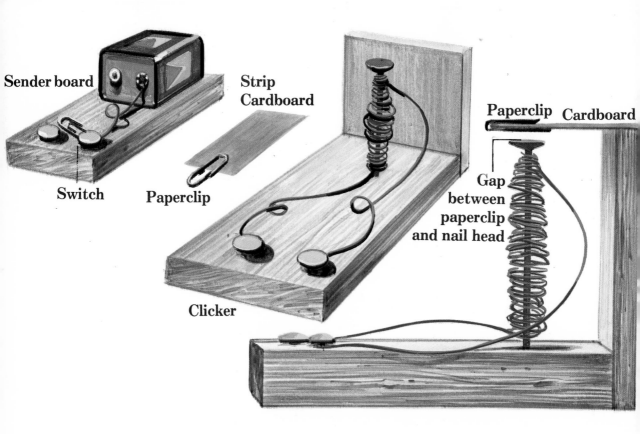

Sender board

Strip
Cardboard

Paperclip   Cardboard

Switch

Paperclip

Gap
between
paperclip
and nail head

Clicker

Telegraph systems make it possible to communicate with people across great distances of land and sea. The early telegraph machines sent their messages using Morse code. You can make a telegraph system to use with a friend. First make a "sender board" using thumbtacks, a paperclip and a battery. Fix the battery to the base board. Connect one terminal of the battery to the switch.

To make a "clicker," hammer a nail

into a piece of wood. Turn the nail into an electromagnet by wrapping wire around it. Fasten the two ends of this wire to the board with thumbtacks. Attach a small piece of wood to the end of the clicker board. This piece of wood should be slightly higher than the head of the nail. Cut a small strip of cardboard. Fasten it to the top of this wooden support. Fix a paperclip onto the cardboard (see illustration) and position it above the nail head. It should not touch the nail.

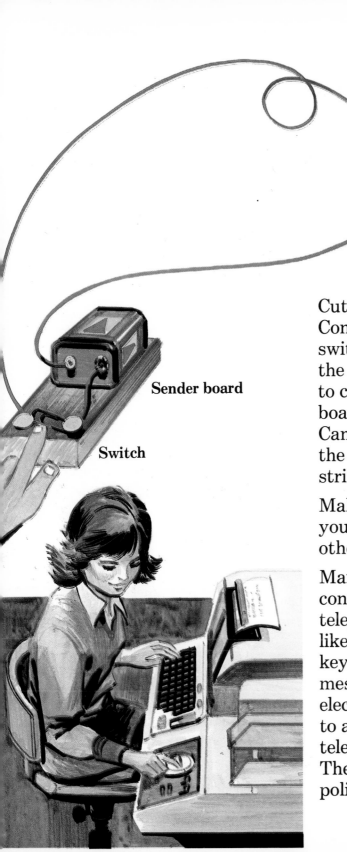

Clicker

Sender board

Switch

Cut two long lengths of wire. Connect one from the sender board switch to one of the thumbtacks on the clicker board. Use the other wire to connect the battery to the clicker board. Press the switch on and off. Can your friend hear the click as the paperclip on the cardboard strikes the electromagnet?

Make another telegraph system for your friend. Communicate with each other from one room to another.

Many telegraph systems are connected to machines called teleprinters. These machines look like typewriters and have a similar keyboard. The sender types out a message which is carried by electricity along the telegraph wires to a receiver machine. This teleprinter types out the message. These systems are used by the police and by newspapers.

15

Using a telephone

Telephones play an important part in our lives today. We use them to talk to our friends and to call for help in emergencies. We can speak to people in many countries around the world.

A telephone handset contains two instruments. The part you speak into is called the mouthpiece or transmitter. We listen to messages through the earpiece or receiver.

The mouthpiece contains granules of carbon and a thin metal disk called a diaphragm. When you speak into the mouthpiece the sound waves from your voice make the metal disk vibrate. These vibrations move the carbon granules. An electric current passes through the granules and is changed by the vibrations. This varying flow of electricity travels along wires to the earpiece of another telephone.

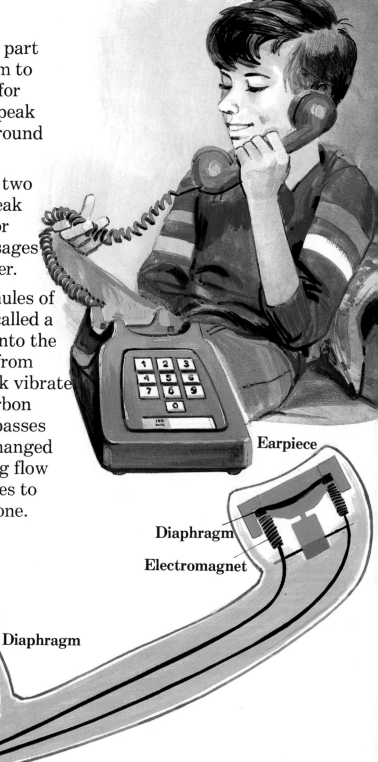

Earpiece

Diaphragm

Electromagnet

Mouthpiece   Diaphragm

Carbon granules

The earpiece contains an electromagnet and a diaphragm. The changing flow of electricity to the electromagnet causes the diaphragm to vibrate. This makes sound waves so that the listener can hear the speaker's voice.

How are people connected to each other? When there are few people using the telephone in an area, they are sometimes connected by a telephone operator. The operator uses a switchboard to connect one caller to another. Many telephone calls are now connected automatically. The caller lifts the handset and hears the dial tone. When the number is dialed it is connected directly. Modern telephone exchanges handle millions of telephone calls. They are designed so that new customers can easily be added to the existing network. Try to visit a telephone exchange.

Telephone exchange

17

Radio waves

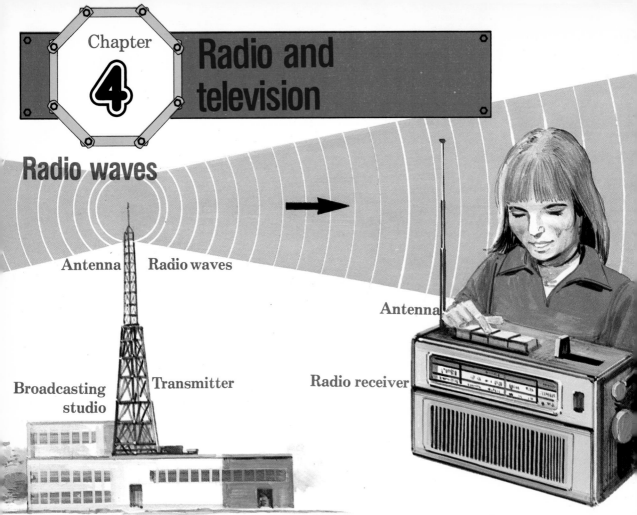

Antenna Radio waves

Antenna

Broadcasting studio

Transmitter

Radio receiver

Listen to a radio. How many different programs can you choose from? You are using a means of communication in which the sender and the receiver are not connected by wires. In fact, it was at one time called a "wireless" because of this.

The sounds that you hear on your radio are first made in a broadcasting studio. These sounds are carried on radio waves sent out from the transmitter antenna of the studio. They may travel hundreds of miles to reach your radio receiver. Scientists describe these radio waves as "electromagnetic waves." They travel at 299,330 km (186,000 miles) per second and are invisible. Radios have antennas to pick up these waves.

Does your radio have an external (outside) antenna? Some modern radios have small antennas built inside the receiver.

18

Radio communications

Radio brings entertainment and information to our homes. We hear the news from all over the world. Often the news is announced as it is happening. We are supplied with weather forecasts and given exact time signals.

Radio is used by many people in their jobs. The police use small "walkie-talkie" radios to

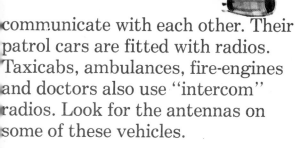

communicate with each other. Their patrol cars are fitted with radios. Taxicabs, ambulances, fire-engines and doctors also use "intercom" radios. Look for the antennas on some of these vehicles.

Radio messages are sent to ships from ashore, and ships can communicate with us even from the middle of the oceans. Airplanes are guided from airport to airport, and even use radio signals to land in poor weather.

Can you think of other ways we use radio?

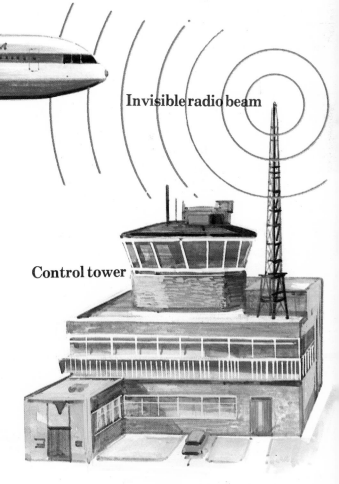

Invisible radio beam

Control tower

Television

Television is a miracle of the
modern world. Not only can we hear
what is happening many, many miles
away, but we can actually see it.
Television cameras follow the event
to be televised. This may be in a
television studio or at a sporting

event in the open air.
The images that the cameras
see are changed into electric
signals. These picture signals,
and signals from the sounds
of the event, are sent out from tall
transmitting antennas. They travel
long distances, as electromagnetic
waves, to the receiver antennas of
television sets. Usually these
antennas are on the roofs of houses.
Look for television aerials near your
home. Other television sets have
antennas on top of the sets.
What happens when you move these
antennas from side to side?

The sound and picture signals arrive at the receiver antenna and travel to the television set.

This receiver now makes a number of changes. The sound signals are changed into sounds which we hear through the loudspeaker of the set. The picture signals are changed into the pictures which we see on the television screen. This is done using a device called a cathode ray tube.

There are now millions of television sets in homes around the world. Television is also used in other ways. Look for small television cameras in large stores. What are they doing? Look for television cameras on buildings above busy road junctions. Why are these cameras being used?

Communications towers

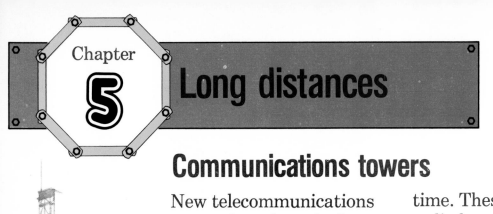

New telecommunications towers have been built to cope with the increase in the use of telephones and television. Some of these towers are over 200 meters (600ft) all. Near the top they have a number of "dish" radio antennas. Each one of these antennas can handle thousands of telephone calls at the same time. These calls travel on radio beams. The beams travel in straight lines. The curvature of the earth means that the towers need to be tall to allow the radio beams to pass directly to other towers. Is there a communications tower near your home? How many "dish" antennas does it have?

Invisible radio beam

Earth

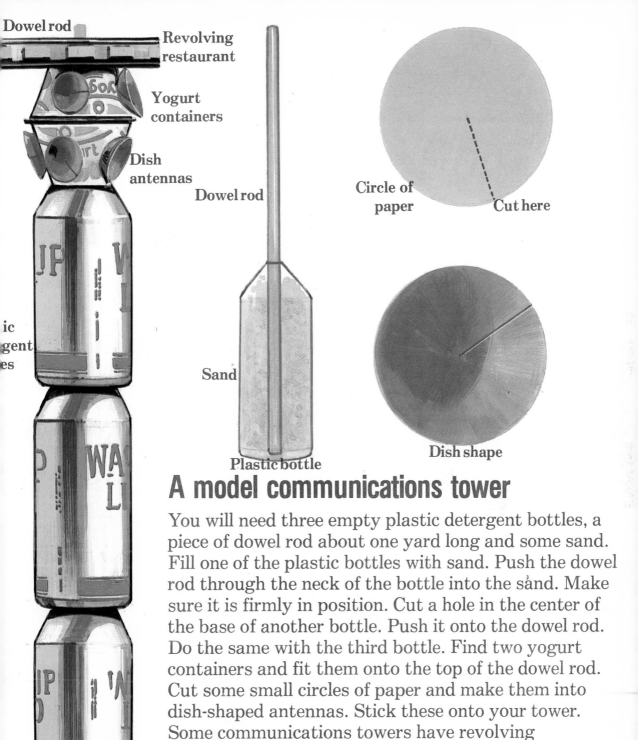

Dowel rod

Revolving restaurant

Yogurt containers

Dish antennas

Dowel rod

Circle of paper

Cut here

ic gent es

Sand

Plastic bottle

Dish shape

A model communications tower

You will need three empty plastic detergent bottles, a piece of dowel rod about one yard long and some sand. Fill one of the plastic bottles with sand. Push the dowel rod through the neck of the bottle into the sand. Make sure it is firmly in position. Cut a hole in the center of the base of another bottle. Push it onto the dowel rod. Do the same with the third bottle. Find two yogurt containers and fit them onto the top of the dowel rod. Cut some small circles of paper and make them into dish-shaped antennas. Stick these onto your tower. Some communications towers have revolving restaurants. Make one for your model using two circles of cardboard. Paint your tower. Could you fit a flashing light on the top?

23

Under the sea

A network of communications cables lies beneath the seas of the world. Over one hundred years ago, the first successful cable was laid under the Atlantic, joining Britain and the U.S.A. Now many countries are joined by such cables under the Pacific, Atlantic and Indian Oceans. It is not easy to lay cables in stormy seas. Special cable-laying ships are now used. The cables themselves also need to be protected from damage by the sea. A new hazard to these cables are the oil-rigs drilling on the sea-bed. New pipelines have to be laid and sometimes these can damage communications cables. Engineers must plan carefully so that expensive and difficult repairs are not needed.

Satellites

Today we live in the Space Age. Powerful rockets are built and men travel into space. These rockets are also used to put satellites into orbit around the earth. Many of these satellites are used for communications.

Most communications satellites are placed in a stationary orbit: they travel in space at the same speed at which the earth rotates, so they are always above the same place on the earth's surface. They are used to send telephone calls and television pictures across the world. Have you ever watched a television program that was being sent by satellite across the world?

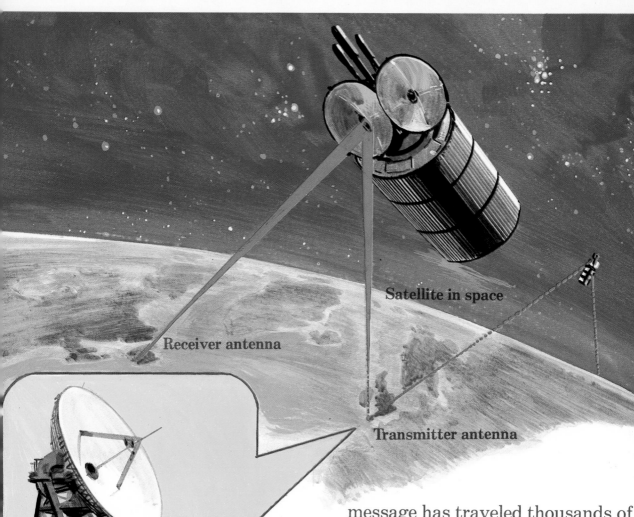

Satellite in space

Receiver antenna

Transmitter antenna

Radio signals are sent to communications satellites from earth stations. These communications stations have large dish-shaped antennas. Look for one near your home or when you are on vacation. When a satellite receives a message from a transmitter antenna, the message has traveled thousands of miles and may be quite weak.

The satellite strengthens the signal before they are beamed back to the receiver antennas on earth. One satellite will be dealing with hundreds of telephone calls at the same time.

To put satellites into space is expensive. They are so useful that their cost is often shared by a number of countries.

A model communications system

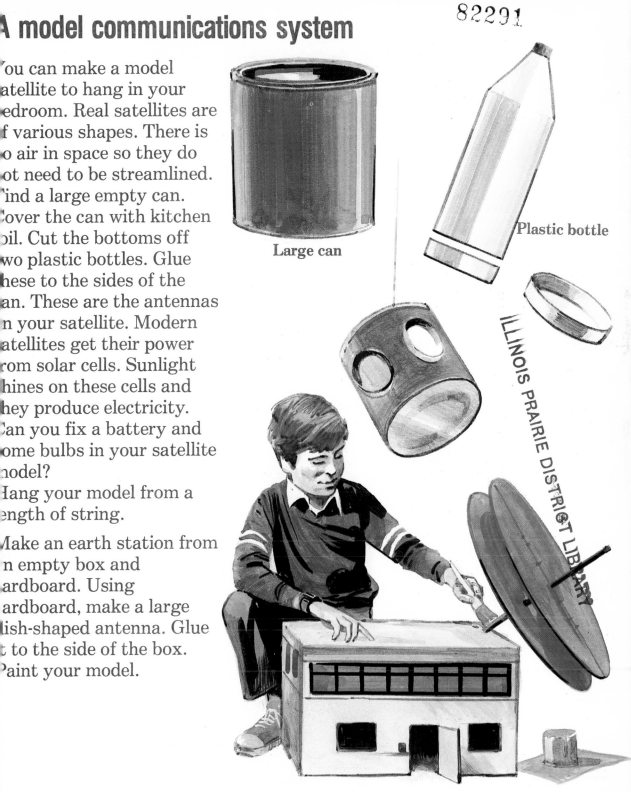

You can make a model satellite to hang in your bedroom. Real satellites are of various shapes. There is no air in space so they do not need to be streamlined. Find a large empty can. Cover the can with kitchen foil. Cut the bottoms off two plastic bottles. Glue these to the sides of the can. These are the antennas on your satellite. Modern satellites get their power from solar cells. Sunlight shines on these cells and they produce electricity. Can you fix a battery and some bulbs in your satellite model?

Hang your model from a length of string.

Make an earth station from an empty box and cardboard. Using cardboard, make a large dish-shaped antenna. Glue it to the side of the box. Paint your model.

Large can

Plastic bottle

Microchips

At one time, many of the machines used in communications contained tubes. These were large, got very hot and were unreliable. But they were important in controlling the electricity in the machines. Can you find an old radio tube?

Later, transistors were invented. These were smaller and lasted longer than tubes.

Do you have a transistor radio? It is much smaller than an old radio which used tubes.

The invention of the integrated circuit or "microchip" has made the future of communications very exciting. One microchip can contain thousands of tiny transistors. These transistors are linked together into electric

Transistor

Tube

Silicon chip

Plastic case

circuits on "chips" of a material called silicon. Some of these silicon chips are so small they can pass through the eye of a needle. The silicon chip, with the integrated circuit, is fitted into a small plastic case. This makes it easier to handle.

Engineers use microchips in many types of communications machinery.

28

Computers

Computers can help us to handle information. Tubes were used to build the first computers. Engineers then used transistors, but the invention of silicon chips has made computers less expensive, smaller

Screen

Keyboard

and more powerful. At home, or in school, you may have a microcomputer.

It has a keyboard so that you can type instructions to the computer. A screen shows what you have typed. The facts that you type into the computer can be stored on magnetic tape in a cassette or on a floppy disk".

Some children use microcomputers

to help them with their lessons in school. Teachers write computer programs and store them on the cassette tapes or floppy disks. These can then be used by different children at various times.

Small computers can be used to communicate information to us. Can you think of ways we could use them in school and at home?

Databanks

Computers are good at storing information, or data, and sorting it out very quickly. More and more information is being stored in the databanks of computers. Governments use computers to store information on their citizens. Banks keep details of their customers' accounts in computer memories. Police forces store details of criminals and stolen cars in the databanks of their computers.

Modern computers store data on magnetic tapes or disks, but even better memories are being developed. This means that a lot of facts can be stored in a small place. There is no need to use paper or filing cabinets. But most important when someone needs information it can be found very quickly by the computer. Can you think of ways in which databanks might help you in school?

Databank

Receiver

Transmitter

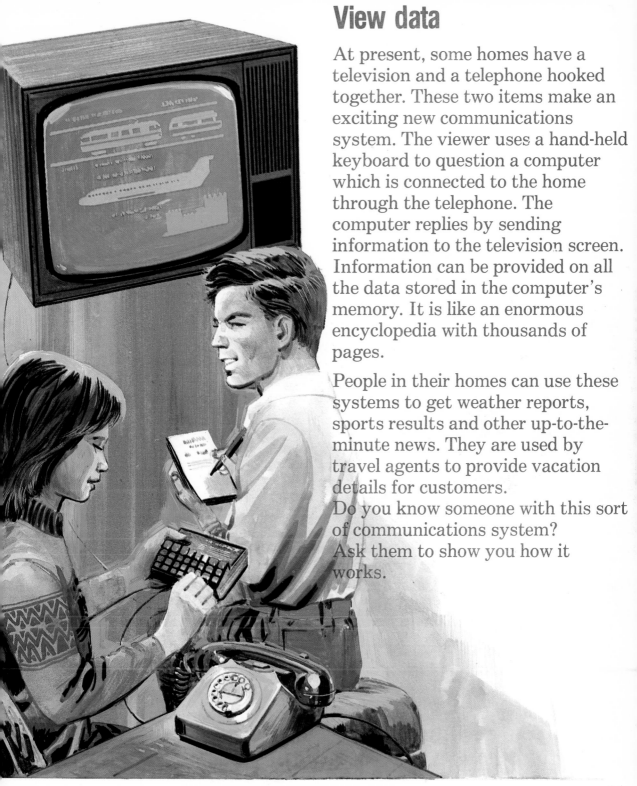

View data

At present, some homes have a television and a telephone hooked together. These two items make an exciting new communications system. The viewer uses a hand-held keyboard to question a computer which is connected to the home through the telephone. The computer replies by sending information to the television screen. Information can be provided on all the data stored in the computer's memory. It is like an enormous encyclopedia with thousands of pages.

People in their homes can use these systems to get weather reports, sports results and other up-to-the-minute news. They are used by travel agents to provide vacation details for customers.
Do you know someone with this sort of communications system?
Ask them to show you how it works.

Optical fibers

Networks of new communications cables are now being laid. These cables are made of the purest glass and are no thicker than a human hair. Engineers call these cables "optical fibers".

One optical fiber cable can carry thousands of telephone calls at the same time. Eight fibers, measuring less than 1cm (½in) in diameter, can carry 8,000 calls. This means that it will be less expensive to use the telephone and to send television pictures and computer information.

Messages are sent along the cables using pulses of light instead of electricity. These light pulses are made using lasers. Watch for engineers fitting optical fibers into underground ducts. Notice how easily they can handle the fibers. What do they do to make the fibers run easily into the ducts?